POEMS
FOR AMERICA

WILLIAM OWENS

Copyright © 2017 by William Owens

All rights reserved. Any resemblance of illustrations to actual persons, living or dead, or actual events is purely coincidental. No part of this publication may be reproduced, distributed, or transmitted in any form or by any means, including photocopying, recording, or other electronic or mechanical methods, without the prior written permission of the publisher, except in the case of brief quotations embodied in critical reviews and certain other noncommercial uses permitted by copyright law.

Printed in the United States of America

ISBN 978-1-64008-893-1

Published by:
Through People Publishers
www.throughpeople.com

TABLE OF **CONTENTS**

INTRODUCTION	7
AMERICA IN TROUBLE	9
PRAYER AS AN AMERICAN	12
CRUCIBLE OF TRANSITION	13
SUPERFICIAL LIBERTY	15
I KILLED A MOSQUITO	18
RAGE TO ROSES	20
TAP OUT	24
SILENCE IS CONSENT	25
THE AMERICAN MAN	29
ENLARGE OUR HEARTS	33
THE BIRTH OF THE USA	37
DEEP CHOCOLATE	38
GOD IS NEAR	40
PUSH THROUGH IT	42
HAIR DYE	43
THE NARRATIVE	44
PEACE • LIBERTY • FREEDOM	47
THE SILENT KNOWING	48
STAND	50
A FALSE SAFE	52

RESIST	54
DON'T YOU DARE DWINDLE	55
REALLY LIVING	57
DEFUSED	58
THREE	59
THE LORD TRIETH	61
WEALTH, POVERTY AND POLITICS	63
THEY ARE WATCHING ME	67
RHETORIC PREVAILS	68
RESET	71
THE RHYTHM OF THE LEAVES	74
PERCEPTION	76
HEMORRHAGE	78
PURGE	79
I'M TIRED	81
PROVOKED	83
SIGH	87
TIME	88
CONSCIENCE	89
OH GOD	94
BUMPS	96
MY WHOLE HEART	98
THE FINISH LINE	100
THE NEXT DAY	101
A JOYOUS GAZE	103

COMPOSURE	104
I GOT TO	106
THE FIELD OF BLOOD	108
BIRDS AT EASE	111
GET FREE	112
THE FINISH LINE	113

Special Poems That Speaks To Our Hearts and Our Nation

PERCEPTION	117
IMPLICIT TRUST	119
I GOT TO	122
PRESS	124
WAIT	125
REFUGEE	127
SHIFT TO GREATNESS	131

INTRODUCTION

POEMS FOR AMERICA *began as one poem - America in Trouble. It was written as an expression of deep pain and a revelation that our nation was in trouble as I witnessed the senseless killings of Americans and our first responders during the presidential election of 2016. I was simply horrified to think that our leading world nation would go to such deplorable levels to deal with internal conflicts and differences. Regardless of the offenses, the taking of life, disregard for authority and respect for citizens, were a reflection upon our nation's leaderships' inability to handle conflict, civil unrest and systemic injustices without the rhetoric of condemnation and accusation to in many ways to simply deflect the blame. This chosen path, often fueled by media spin and prejudice, would only ignite the people to act destructively rather than taking the higher ground towards resolution and reconciliation by calm response not heated reaction.*

Even more troubling was the eerie silence from within the ranks of spiritual leadership that possessed the large platforms to influence goodness, love and calmness during this painful time. While there were many who did intervene on local levels, many "gate keepers" of the cities, states and of the nation could have done more. That deliberate silence—an omission of spiritual responsibility—revealed a deep disconnection between spiritual leadership and the trouble that faced our nation during this time. It was an opportunity missed by "the servants" whose God founded this nation.

The poet's pen tapped my heart again and again and the words were given to me that captured each event for these days. From the lobbies of hotels, the tables of restaurants and even my car during different times of the day and of the night, I wrote a poem every day until 53 days had passed, ending on the day of the presidential election. I even shared these poems with people and captured their responses on video which where posted on Instagram and Facebook. You can view them at www.poetsforamerica.com

These poems represent an unapologetic appeal to God for mercy upon America and a call to each of us to return to faith in Him and loving our neighbor as ourselves and even our enemies. We overcome evil with good.

I believe you will be challenged, refreshed and encouraged.

Do not be overcome by evil, but overcome evil with good. Romans 12:21

William Owens
North Hollywood, CA
May 2017

AMERICA IN TROUBLE

September 14, 2016

America is in Trouble
Doubled over in pain
From the insane parcels of problems
That have rearranged our land

Disdainful debates replace the kind and respectful
Conversations we used to have
It was okay to disagree
But together we still watched football
On the big screen TV
...back in the day

Now the players refuse to stand
For the country that gives them the freedom
To play on the field of dreams
Getting paid to amaze their fans
Living life grand - unlike most of us
Who work hard to make ends meet day by day
Instead they choose to grandize what fractures us
Rather than discovering what could connect us
In the end zone of hope on which the touchdown of love
And the field goal of unity is made

There is a playbook that would show a strategy
To stand and pledge for our country and take us all higher
While making whoever lives they believe matter still matter
...even more

Politicians are people like us
With motives and agendas
Except we scrutinize with a public eye
They get exposed live

We vote after our own heart's desire
Who can cast the first stone
We as Americans are humans
And have all lied, about to lie or are liars all the time
To ourselves the most
And yet we boast that this politician will lead us into bliss
So we kiss their hand
And make them our king or the first queen

America is in Trouble
Because we really believe that politics will save the day
Even some that dishonor the USA

To the God of which our nation is under, I say we pray
For all lives and wounded hearts to be healed
Only then will this deep, self-inflicted, agonizing pain
That has America in Trouble and doubled over
gradually go away
Giving way to the prophetic words of Martin Luther King

Let freedom ring
Let freedom ring

Should God show us mercy, these days will pass
We then will also rejoice with King
Declaring
Thank God Almighty
We are free at last

Scan the QR code with your phone and experience the video or audio of this poem performed by William Owens.

PRAYER AS AN AMERICAN

September 15, 2016

Prayer is the heart's cry
For an honest desire in wanting to know why
To grasp the significance of so much pain

To press pass the insane battles
Of our days and of our lives
To melt away the anxieties that paralyze our smile
Turning it into an angry frown that's upside down

We as Americans don't really pray
We just complain to God about not having our way
To pray is to ask the God – under whom this nation stands –
What He wants with you – what's His plan
Only then can you humbly pray to discover the wisdom
Of His ways and the courage fulfill His will and simply obey

Remember, you are a child of God and a citizen
of His Kingdom
A pilgrim passing through
Set your affections on things above

Fan into flames your first love
And your prayers as an American
Will revolve around His Kingdom
Pray... again

****

Scan the QR code with
your phone and
experience the video

CRUCIBLE OF TRANSITION

September 16, 2016

Transitions force positions that demand one's attention
Painful contradictions
That offer no rhyme or reason
As to the reality of the intrusion
Of ideologies, philosophies and the
Selfish orientations that only prove what's not right

Not in terms of mere opinionated explanations
But rather in real life consequences
Has it become that hard to see the truth?
1 plus 1 will always be 2!

This trip has caused confusion
And therefore created contusions too numerous to mention
America has become black and blue
Being bruised in practically every sector of society
Education, our national debt, race relations and especially the family

There's simply no explanation as to why our nation
Is being exposed to this radiation of poison that's taking its toll

We've departed from the old paths of standards
That kept such atrocities like this from happening
We've ceased to pay attention to the God of this nation
Who raised us to this place of exaltation

We are in a free fall from the stagnation of compromise
To satisfy our own hearts' desires
This transition has exposed the leaders of this
Paradoxical conundrum
Of old failed socialism… habitual liars

For all things good we no longer seem useful
God therefore has placed us in a crucible that will try us sorely
A transition that will prove us deeply

Will America endure and fight for righteousness another day?
Or succumb to the wicked hand of this deceitful grip
around her neck?
One answer will determine that

Will the Americans who love America bow their knees
And pray to the God who made this US of A?

Only then will this crucible prove useful
If we fail, this transition will be the end
Of what we used to call our nation

****

Scan the QR code with
your phone and experience
the video or audio of this

SUPERFICIAL LIBERTY

September 17, 2016

Superficial Liberty is like food that you feel in your mouth
Yet with no taste to satisfy the buds on your tongue with
flavor and spice

It's like you're moving but never seem to arrive
Your liberty seems to evaporate a bit at a time

A liberty that's accidental
Should be intentional
Revered, appreciate, defended and not taken for granted

Are we a nation truly at liberty?
Or are we prisoners of pleasure
Hoarding up treasures
Always wanting perfect weather
Yelling at people "whatever"!
Just because you're angry that your liberty
Isn't working to make you happy

We want our food, to have fun with no need to worry
About the sickening void that makes our hearts heavy
Always seem to be stressing

We can't wait to celebrate
Throw a party to simply escape

Eat our steaks that sizzle
While deep inside our soul we feel the gnawing conviction
That we are hypocritical and superficial

Possessions are a false worth
No matter how big your purse
America was not founded to only have a house on a lake
History tells us the pilgrims also came to worship
In freedom and liberty to express their faith

Such things are a blessing to possess
We must never think, however, they will give us the rest
for our weary souls, our bored lives
Frustrated and undefined passions
that drive us to an early grave
with nothing more than a confession of faith
In God, we say

The depth of our liberty has become a shallow, hallow pit
That's been reduced to no more than how we live
And especially what we eat
No longer using liberty to pursue the why that calls to us
From within the depths of our souls.
Many of us haven't even taken the time to know
What that even is

I compel you
Plead with you
Provoke you

To break away from the superficiality
That has created a false reality
Of those lives we see displayed on TV for all to see
Most ending in tragedy

Possess your soul
Your mind
Your spirit
Embrace what's real

Resist the temptation for things
Recapture the flame for your faith
Seek to advance things eternal
that shall have no end

Release
Realign
Redeem
The time
...Is short

I KILLED A MOSQUITO

September 18, 2106

I killed a mosquito in my car
It wanted to suck me dry
Of the blood that gives me life

I slammed it against the windshield
With the palm of my hand
It's still there in my car totally dried
I keep it there to remind me
That I don't have to be afraid of a pest
That seeks to disturb the rest of my soul
To trouble me that I would have a wreck
While I drive down the road

Why have we as a nation allowed an insect
To cause us to react like beasts?
Killing, burning and acting without dignity
Believing we're better than others
For no reason
We've been blinded by pride
Thinking we're justified by a narrative told us
...It was a lie

It buzzes in our ear
Stings us
Creates an itch

Throws us in a fit
We drive into a ditch
That's stupid

We fail to see just how small this mosquito is
No real threat
If we simply slammed it against
Our windshield
It'd be dead

We are not that mosquito
But if we let it bite us
We in turn become it
May we kill this blood-sucking contagious insect
Our souls' pest
With the only repellant that gives us a strong immunity
It's potent ingredients are hope, love & unity

Spray it on your heart and share it generously
That mosquito will veer away from you
Instead, butterflies will welcome your presence
And so will heaven
For such are the children of God
... now I'll go ahead and wipe my windshield off
Of that which is dead and gone

****

Scan the QR code with your phone and experience the video or audio of this poem performed by William Owens.

RAGE TO ROSES

September 19, 2016

There is a rage within our nation
A swelling of hidden frustrations from seeds of injustices
Atrocities justified by twisted philosophies
That were simply inhuman

From the history of slavery
Upon the most glorious of creation
To systemic in-your-face racism that creates complication
Of finding community that will celebrate your vision
What's worse is when that nation fails to pay attention
For centuries and still counting

Rage is building an army of disproportioned people
Whose hearts are bruised
From being used regardless of their pigmentation
Lives being shattered
It's no wonder oppressed people demand
To know their lives matter
To themselves more than others
It's hard to keep breathing under the cover of
"One day my change gonna come"

Frederick Douglas spoke words that resound today
He said, "When any class is made to feel that society
Is an organized conspiracy to oppress, rob and degrade them,
Neither person nor property will be safe"

Before that, however, he makes plan that
"Where justice is denied, where poverty is enforced,
Where ignorance prevails;" he was telling us that
Making lives matter works both ways

We the oppressed have to stand above the oppressor
We have to do and be better
We must stand for all that's right
Never lose sight of the rights to our nation
But use our freedom to turn the tide in favor of all men
Resist the envy, jealousy and the quest to cause unrest
Lead with hope, love and unity fueled by the force
of forgiveness

Lincoln was prophetic in his resolve to fight against slavery
He saw the iniquity of the nation would bring
consequences
This principle he chose to stand for
Even at the cost of a bloody civil war
He declared, "America will never be
Destroyed from the outside
If we falter and lose our freedoms
It will be because we destroyed ourselves"

Men of old knew what we still fail to know
Our pride is feeding this rage in the soul
We refuse to recognize that none of us are alone
A nation is responsible for her own
We willfully fall, continue to fail, and will always falter

If we refuse to love our sister and our brother
We are family
We are Americans

The pressure is building
We must address this quiet rage
That can explode into civil unrest
A fire will spread from coast to coast
Unrestrained anger will be out of control

We can correct this
If we commit to a higher way
Be like Jesus and forgive our enemy
Resolve to resist the taking of life
Every soul has the God-given right to live
and not die

Rage can be replaced with rest
If we reset
Rage can be deflated
If we become obligated
To ourselves regardless of the past
We are free from the judgments and acts of society
We see the silver in the clouds and work to make it brighter
For everyone to see

Rage can give birth to roses overnight
When we recognize that our fight is not against each other
But an enemy we can't see

Evil spirits and principalities
A foe that most don't know
Or just refuse to believe exists
It is he who plays the strings of wretched music
Laced with wicked lyrics to get us to become delirious

One word will do
Say to him... Satan, the Lord rebuke you!
It will end the rage...
Heal the wounds
Give us grace
Unite our nation
Arrest the frustration
Restore the vision
Of our forefathers like
Frederick Douglass, Martin Luther King, John F. Kennedy
and Abraham Lincoln

Roses are blooming...

Scan the QR code with your phone and experience the video or audio of this poem performed by William Owens.

TAP OUT

September 20, 2016

Will America tap out from the pain of the strong hold that won't let go?
Or will she fight from within the core of her soul
To resist the threat
To refuse to retreat
To find strength to get back on her feet?

The moment has arrived for her to decide
America can arise
Be better than before
Resist this evil agenda to make her fold

May God provide America another season to return
This nation back under Him
If she refuses this time
This will be America's last round
Please America, stand up and fight
Don't you dare tap out

SILENCE IS CONSENT

September 21, 2016

Where are the Black preachers who taught divine wisdom
Urging their members to give to another agenda?
As they teach about forgiveness
What are they doing to set an example
In the face of the rising rage in our nation?

They consent to the destructive behavior of Black Lives Matter
When they remain silent
Do they really care about what's happening?
People are dying!

Preachers and leaders must remain true
No matter the hue of the people in front of you
Never surrender to the crowd
Cause your support might have dwindled
We as leaders have been called to live and if necessary die
For a higher principal.

Preachers are needed like never before
To close the door to this hateful agenda
Instead, we've allowed fear of the few to cause us to surrender
Our responsibility – regardless if they look like you
Or sit in your pew

Silence is consent
To the detriment of all people
Such times demand a bold, strong stance to
Confront this attack against our nation... under God
To burn and turn over cars
To throw rocks and burn entire blocks

Perhaps you are afraid of Black Lives Matter
Why?
They need and want your leadership more than ever
Your silence leaves you missing in action
Such silence has closed the door to them listening to sound reason
The relationship you have is nothing more than pretending
That you care about their soul
A true friend will tell the truth
I'm just saying...

I don't see the connection
Of authentic and deep trust with the people you say you lead
They are people no worse or better
Who have the right to believe that their lives matter
They're just looking for a way to weather
This storm of injustice, find peace
And you have it
But your silence is worse than police brutality
'Cause you killing your own people with crude passivity

I'm not against their rage
Indignation can be righteous indeed
I'm feeling their pain and see the need
I just want their methods to be more effective
Thinking they can do whatever will only ignite more violence
They only seem to burn our houses making it difficult to bring peace
Their approach will not make a thing matter and
What happens when they kill more police?
You going to say – it wasn't one of us?
Maybe not, but they still rode on our bus and we didn't even know it

Fact is, it isn't costing you nothing
Or you'd definitely be saying something
Your silence is screaming louder than you can imagine
Because the people are watching and can tell you ain't leading
Your silence is against this wave of rage
That's spreading and gaining momentum

Jesus said, "Forgive them for they know not what they do"
Yea... that doesn't apply to you or me because we say we see!

Break your silence or the blood of many will be
on your hands
I know you see there is a better plan

Forgive the rude and somewhat articulation
of my frustration
I only want to see what I know only the preachers do
Love by deeds
Sowing seeds of hope
Examples of unity
This alone will save ours and our neighbor's communities

Consent to Silence No More
Please

Scan the QR code with your phone and experience the video or audio of this poem performed by William Owens.

THE AMERICAN MAN

September 22, 2016

The American man has been faking
His existence
Trying to experience
What he's thinking
Deep inside, he's trapped with
Unfulfilled expectations
Spending His life trying to explain
As to why or to justify
That he's not living his passion

Instead, he's mastered just making a living
A prisoner of things temporal
A false flash of satisfaction
That drains the American man's soul empty
(...every 16 hours)
Sleep about 8 then starts over when he awakes

Some have authority as a cover up for their hypocrisy
Flash a badge, hold an office, some even pastor
Got a gun to demand respect
So the law gives you that....
I pray to God you use it right

Others are outlaws
Bent on a freefall way of living

Simply rebelling
Against the grain
Because of the strain of life
No reprise
To reset
Only regret gone wild

All the while, most men driving what they don't own
Going to work
Saying hi – yet alone
At home he's in a zone
Afraid to really expose his heart
To the one he says he loves
Hoping deeply that she loves him in return

Besides all this, he must recognize it begins with him
The value he has of himself
Regardless of what he or she might say
It goes both ways at the end of the day

The man in you will one day die
But you have opted to live like you're paralyzed
You overanalyze
Rationalize away
The vision you have burning inside

Trapped in a matrix
Where everything is fixed
Told when to awake

and when to go to bed
What to eat
Remain neat
You know there's more
Your soul is telling you so
You instead choose again to ignore
To your heart you close the door

We wonder why our nation has become dry
With aimless pursuits
Lost identity to where the man no longer is relevant
The family being redefined
Become sublime

To a narrative that in time will prove was not right
For the entire nation – not the individual – to be defined
It was an attack on the man
Must be the plan
To redefine our land of the free
The home of the brave
Men these days have become cowards
Afraid to speak truth to power

The most endangered species
Had better fight for his identity
Without the man taking a stand
It will be the end of our America
We say we love so dearly

Man – hear what I say
Regardless of your color
Whoever or whatever
Take your place
Be fearless
Your country cannot be
Without you being true
To yourself

You are the core foundation
On which this nation stands
You are... The American Man

ENLARGE OUR HEARTS

September 23, 2016

Enlarge our hearts
Expand our minds
Beyond the limits of our brains
That constrain us out of fear to maintain
A twisted reasoning that takes us prisoner

In the rusted chains
Of the insane same way of thinking
We've got to go deeper
To save our nation
From the evaporations of hate

The heart of America is fixed
Refuses to move beyond the sick past of yesterday
Hired missionaries keep it that way
They run interference
To create a false appearance
Less we realize our hearts being healed
Is the key that will also heal our nation

We've got no leader
Only men pleasers
Who tease us with false humility
No real intent to create harmony
Only false promises that we swallow

Proves us gullible
Brings us trouble
Again and again

When will we learn
They are not for us?
We are a republic
It is by our voice we live and thrive
Our rights give us power
To remove such people
Who only divide

Our country is not responsible for giving us anything
It provides us opportunities to fulfill our dreams
A republic can only experience its liberty and freedom
As it exercises its heart muscle
To love beyond the reasons
Of injustice and treason
Committed with impunity against us, its citizens

Legislation and the government
Will never give our country rest
Only weigh us down with another tax
Seeking more ways to exact them from us
Giving the elite the right to dictate
A false perspective
Through the media
Who's supposed to report the truth

Without fear of threat?
It's the constitution that gives us freedom of the press

We buy it hook, line and sinker
None the wiser
We keep up their agenda
Because we've allowed our hearts to surrender
To a false narrative and then we wonder… why

We need intervention
To stop this bleeding
Our heart has become smaller
Our will divided
The tension tangible
Our actions reprehensible
We've become cynical, judgmental
Accusers of our neighbor
The solution is not another election of a human
Not an army of smart people thinking that will do better
With no healing within the heart
We will all fall apart
The real solution is that America
Needs the intervention of God!

God has the key to every heart
His power can erase the deep-seated pain
Release the intolerable strain
Uproot the anger that is sweeping our land

Through.... Christ
We can be set free individually

America will not be forever
Her season will surrender to a greater agenda
Only those who would have yielded will be counted worthy
To transition to a new nation that will have no end
A city with streets made of gold
Where peace abides and love overflows
Pain, anger, division and any dark
Intention will be non-existent

That's why America was and why one day she will be no more
To spread truth throughout every nation
God is the only One who can keep us from falling apart
He will do so if we yield to Him to enlarge our hearts

Scan the QR code with your phone and experience the video or audio of this poem performed by William Owens.

THE BIRTH OF THE USA

September 23, 2016

America is the land of the free and the home of the brave
There is a reason why it is this way
It didn't happen for no apparent reason
It was the result of a deep, profound faith that brought
people this way
It was the desire to worship God who gave birth
to the USA

DEEP CHOCOLATE

September 24, 2016

Deep Chocolate is a commitment
To a succulent experience that satisfies
A part of the soul that words fail to expose

It is an experience of emotions that rapture the senses
Exceed expectations beyond reason
Sending pleasure to places not quite understood
And yet it's all good

Layers
Of goodness
Waves of darkness
Compels a full commitment
No room for regret
Not for the timid
To go deeply to where
Only chocolate can take you

We as a nation should have this experience
By declaring a Chocolate Day to remind us that
There is delight when we commit
To the deep, rich and creamy goodness of our nation
That no matter the faults, misdirection and wrong
decisions of the past
We are yet rich

None can compete
Our nation is yet under God
And like chocolate
We are loved
Adored
And enjoyed

Roll your eyes and take another bite
There is no delight in the world like the USA.

Scan the QR code with your phone and experience the video or audio of this poem performed by William Owens.

GOD IS NEAR

September 25, 2016

Let me be clear
That God is drawing near
Nearer than he's even been
It is simply time
For a shift

I sense it in the atmosphere
I see it in the activity around me
I refuse to be blind
Or bend to a lie
Reject the desire to be liked
Only to be led
To a place to where God is not

Evidence is plentiful
To justify that...
God is here
Prepare for a reckoning
A manifestation of the consequences of our decisions
Our opinions
Choice of direction

When God arrives
There be no time

To rectify
Or explain why

Time of grace will be no more
God is nearer
Than He's ever been
It is soon to be the end as we know it
... and then eternity...

Hallelujah!

PUSH THROUGH IT

September 26, 2016

Push through the pain
The cold rain
That pours upon your brain
And even drains
Your heart
Making you want to quit the fight
To fold, to retreat

Just breathe
Reflect on the truth
Reject voices of condemnation
Rest and remember His faithfulness
Think only for the day

Tomorrow will arrive on time
You'll keep the faith again
Embrace He who embraces you
You are not alone
In this journey
In this nation
Let hope, love and unity
Be your contemplation

Push through it

HAIR DYE

September 27, 2016

We dye our hair to hide the gray that stains our image
Makes old our appearance

We dye our hearts with shows of false jesters
No matter the reason

Be yourself
Resist the temptation
To be non authentic

America
Need only be herself
Every shade
Tribe and language
You are family
No dye or reason why
Just be American
No need ever again for that old can of hair dye

THE NARRATIVE

September 28, 2016

It's imperative that we follow the right narrative
That we refuse to get distracted from the facts
That project upon us truth
Though they be lies

We get lost in between the lines
Because we are all too often surprised
With what's happening
When we shouldn't be
Jesus said it would come to pass this way
So why are we acting crazy?

The narrative is a position of convictions
That are deeply embedded in our hearts
It's the things that we believe are true
No matter how far we go
To discover what we think we know

To hold to the narrative that will endure
One must be held by its author and creator
It's not enough to think you understand its voice

Because you hear the words
You must be owned by them
Captured in imagination

Raptured you in a deep commitment
Without it, you are subject to its controlling agenda

There are only two
One is true
The other is lie
One will give life
The other will ensure you die
The one who speaks the truth is all that matters

He is giver of life
The author and the finisher
The mighty redeemer
No other narrative actually even matters

Yield
Align your mind
To the truth that's living
It will speak through you
A narrative that is relevant
Freeing
Liberating
And final

The narrative I speak of is the only one
That has resurrecting power...

Our nation needs this narrative more than any other
It is the only one that can heal

Cause us to recover
Create a wholeness within our hearts
Open our eyes to behold the truth
And restart afresh
This is the only narrative that will give the
United States of America
A much-needed rest

Scan the QR code with your phone and experience the video or audio of this poem performed by William Owens.

PEACE • LIBERTY • FREEDOM

September 29, 2016

Peace is the application of Christ upon our hearts
Liberty is a divine interruption into the chaos all around
Freedom is a God imparted state of being that
no man, woman
Or nation can extract from those who have it
within the depths
Of their soul and they won't let go
These three are for the brave, the free and the strong
Not in self, in religion nor in others
But in God and only through Christ alone

THE SILENT KNOWING

Friday, September 30, 2016

We know when no one is around
When there is an absence of sound
Because deep down inside
Conviction abounds telling us what is true
What we should do

Despite the contrary winds that seek
To persuade us to yield to what we feel
There is a silent knowing of the truth
That convicts you
Demands of you though no one is talking
It testifies that God is aware
That He is near
That He cares

Yield America to the knowing that
He is speaking in each of our souls
We need not hear sounds that make noise
There is a sound that is deeper still
It speaks
It reaches into the deepest corridors hidden yet real
Only accessible by God

May those who have ears to hear be resolved
To pay attention to His voice

Not heard by ears of flesh
Instead discern with an open heart

This will heal the land
Give grace to forgive
Courage to withstand the hate
For the truth liberates
Love obligates us to show by forgiving
This is the truth and the power of the Silent Knowing.

STAND

Saturday, October 1, 2016

We must stand until our nation grasps
The significance of who we are
In the mind of God
Not mere man

Less we seek after that which cannot fill the void
With a noise that robs us of simple peace

Oh deliver us from being paranoid by the countless
Pointless vain distractions
That add nothing to our country
Only offer interruptions of ideas and suggestions
That have proven to be worth nothing...in the end
Only more destruction

If we stand
We acknowledge our dependency on Him
We confront our deepest pain with truth alone
No need to perform
Just honest confessions of where we are

Refuse to justify what's not working
Yield to His perfect love
Ceaseless power
Amazing grace, how sweet the sound

That saved
It shall and will again
Save our nation
If we simply stand
For Him

A FALSE SAFE

Sunday, October 2, 2106

Shall we be safe in a false place?
Shall we abandon truth for a familiar face?
We damn ourselves with apostasy
Change our name to Ichabod
When we depart from the living God

Where does that put America?
We wonder why such trouble has doubled down
on our nation
Why progress is overcome with stagnation
While we appear to be safe
All the while we are fake
Seen as a divided nation

Fake in our appearance of peace
Property defined by possessions we don't even own
Most being ninety days from losing their home

It's the American way –
Create an appearance of safe
Say you're doing okay
Even though your heart is about to break
From carry this burden to look okay

We as American are in serious trouble living in bubbles
That have names like debt, race, education and
political disgrace

But will we?
Has the time of Grace ended?
Do we keep on pretending?

We are in desperate need of a realignment with the One
Who set us straight to begin with
Only God can remove the fake safe and fix this… only God
I pray we get back under
His loving covering
For the time of reckoning will demand the consequences
That will set things straight
We must all give an account

Now's the time to turn around
Remove the fake
Return to the only safe place…
God, with or without the USA

Scan the QR code with your phone and experience the video or audio of this poem performed by William Owens.

RESIST

Monday, October 3, 2016

Resist the act of the urge that comes
To disturb your peace
That seeks to distract you
From the purpose within your heart

Connected to why you were born
Right where you are
To fulfill your destiny no matter how high
Or far.... it might appear to be

You will have to resist the tempter
And finish what you were put here for
Be strong and Resist
It is merely a test

DON'T YOU DARE DWINDLE

Saturday, October 8, 2106

Life can hit you hard
Take the breath out your lungs
Rattle your brain with strenuous images of insane
Imaginations that tell you to quit

Your life is not legit
To just dwindle away and hide
From the pursuit of why you were made
Made to thrive

What's up with you?
How dare you talk like that as if
It's okay
God made you for a destiny
To fulfill a purpose
Before the foundations of the world
It was to be this way

Don't let the fire in your soul dwindle out to be no more
It is then that you must fight
Resist the lure that's lying to you
Stand against the pressing wind of the devil
Who's afraid more so than you think

Now Arise
America
And return to your God
The idol you have in your hand
Is that which has dwindled you down
Get up and turn around
For not too many days we must give a full account of our lives
Our freedom
Our liberties
Such has been our responsibilities
We must finish strong
Till we behold His face
Brighter than the Sun

We are a finisher
And we never, ever, ever will be a dwindler!

REALLY LIVING

Sunday, October 9, 2016

Really Living is beyond the pale, stale accumulation of things
Of trying to rearrange your life only for the temporal realm

It's not steak and the sizzle
As you drizzle in the fizzle of fleshy pleasure and stored up treasure
Thinking you can do whatever

Really Living is the tangible expression of the will of heaven
It's the connection of God in you, through you to others
To be made whole from the grip of pain upon their soul

Living really is another way to see it
Because it's proof that you are legitimate

America can once again experience the Really Living experience
If she humbly repents and returns under Him... God

DEFUSED

Monday, October 10, 2016

America has been defused from what made her great
She's misused God's grace
Abused the liberty and freedom granted by God for her to
watch over and protect as a steward
Instead, she's turned away
Denied Him the honor and the glory due His name....
This is a shame at what has been displayed.
Oh God, have mercy upon this US of A

THREE

Tuesday, October 11, 2016

We count to three for everything
Taking pictures or the pace to start a song to sing
Begin a race or make a point worth remembering
Three is more than two, less than four
But for some reason these numbers we ignore

Since three has captured our attention, I want to use it
To arrest your affection
That instead you give yourself
To reflection three times a day

Pray for hope to burst like a star within your heart
To fuel your passion to achieve the impossible
To scale a defiant mountain
Pray for love to come upon your being
To redirect your thinking
Compel you to start giving it away in jars
Like cold, sweet lemonade

Pray for unity
To return to the center of our communities
To eradicate hate and disharmony
That makes us phony to ourselves
Then each other...

These are your three times a day prayers
I know it will work you closer to the Lord our God

1, 2, 3 -
Now START!

THE LORD TRIETH

Wednesday, October 12, 2016

He sits above the atmosphere
So very far
And yet so near
Beholding every life so dear
Especially those who want Him

Lover of soul so deep
Presence so sweet
Yet our country tis of thee
Has rejected His tenderness
Refused His kindness

Bliss of favor divine upon our land of liberty
Freedom from sea to sea
We've yet ridiculed Him
The Lord who trieth with fire
Will now try thee

Trouble we've not known
Sorrow dare not show
We are silly doves
Who sold our souls
And does not know the trying
Of our hearts that's before us

God tries the heart
Tests the faithful
Teaches with examples
Of frustration and purpose within us
Lover of soul so deep
Presence so sweet
Yet our country tis of thee
Have ridiculed His tenderness

Bliss of favor divine upon our land of liberty
Freedom from sea to sea
We've yet rejected Him
The Lord who trieth with fire
Will now try thee?

~ Hosea 11:3-4

WEALTH, POVERTY AND POLITICS

Thursday, October 13, 2016

What ingredients create systemic mind sets
What words control the narrative
What ideas herd the people into a zip code
With noise orchestrated not to make sense?

Why in America is it like this?
When there is no chain around anyone's neck
Nor shackles on one's feet
Not being forced to eat what you don't want to eat
Yet people are screaming racism

Of course, it's there
Will always be
This is not heaven
It's a fallen planet working out its salvation
For those who've been called, chosen and soon elevated

Slavery was an evil plan
Killed and maimed
Raped and pillaged minds and bodies
America built on Black backs and others of course

It's not color or pigmentation
America is an organization
A structure and a system of more than just opinions
It's policy, networks and crazy algorithms
People, parties, controlled chaos
unless you pay attention to the right narrative
Who's your boss?

Wealth is more than money
It's a funnel to keep it flowing in a certain direction
By people who are privileged
Privilege is not what you think or necessarily who you know
Nor is it determined by where or to whom you were born

It's about distribution of solutions
Owning the blueprint
Creating with intent
Networking with happiness
Attracting people who like you
Avoiding souls who feed on the past
Of all that's dead

Wealth is waiting for those who listen and pay attention
Knowing they can be adopted into its transition
It doesn't care what color you are

Or you remain in a stagnate orientation of always complaining
Who told you who you are anyway?
And how far you can run?

Who you can be
What you believe
When to achieve
How to dream

Poverty is likened to an analogy of knowledge ignored
Libraries galore
Internet without limit to absorb understanding
But instead you're playing another game on TV
And you're thirty-three
Got nerves to jump on a bus, to fuss on a street
Screaming that your (whatever color you are) lazy life matters
Show me right where you stand that it does

Politics keeps it all legit so they say
Holding people hostage won't let them breathe
Controlled by a narrative about chains
Women being raped
And black men hanged
Again and again
Can they think of another movie to produce instead?
True that... tell the history
But for God's sake, think about your own story
Like did they die in vain
Only for you to complain about why they died?
They be better honored if you thrived instead of just survived

Yea, survive
Hired pipers who look like you
Are getting paid

To keep your mind deranged with what's past
You know who they are
Always fussing and getting paid

Showing up after the Black man is dead, done and in the morgue
Suing the city to get paid – Blood money is what it is – a dangerous game
They keep you there
Less you recognize that you are the you that you want to be
Choose...
Will it be wealth or poverty
the common or spirituality?

It's time for a shift to where wealth is
Not where it's promised
Or will you be the victim again played and made sick
With the controlling, deceptive methods of dumb and deceptive politics?

Not this year.
Lord help us...
We, the people!

Scan the QR code with your phone and experience the video or audio of this poem performed by William Owens.

THEY ARE WATCHING ME

Friday, October 14, 2016

They're watching me
Who I am
What I'm doing
Where I'm going
What I'll be

Whether for threat or a benefit to society
Independent thinker or a perfect member for the group
Who has surrendered their conscience to belong
Afraid to be alone

They are watching me
But fail to realize my Daddy above is watching them

I'm free
Watch on

RHETORIC PREVAILS

Saturday, October 15, 2016

The prescription for depression of most Americans
Is to be obligated
To an overrated ideology that cannot be
Substantiated by history
It's sheer philosophy concocted with phraseologies
That avoid accountability to the people

With cultic rituals
Political agendas
Master pretenders
Complicit leaders
Group thinkers
It's impossible to have a simple conversation

Rhetoric is the new religion
It has a pace that's predictable
A face that familiar
A race of many shades that's gullible

Some ask how and why this can be
Overrule the mind of reason
Common sense and the consequences
Of failures that all can see
Yet rhetoric still prevails

It's conditioning that started decades ago
The first step was when they took prayer out of schools
Rejected God from being mentioned on the job
The Ten Commandments from the court houses near and far
Getting sued for not baking a cake to marry two...

Fear has won the day upon most
Created slaves that are doped
In the brain
Worse than chains
Touching every class of man

People dare not stand alone
Upon the foundation of truth
Needs no voting booth
Was here before America was
Will remain when this nation is dissolved

Rhetoric is weak
Preys upon those who refuse to seek... the truth
Can't stand where there is light
Like a cockroach it scatters
Like a mouse it hides

Eventually it will prevail no more
Those who are its victims
Will lose their very souls

Rhetoric is a convoluted lie
A damn lie
Or statistics
Taken for the gospel as the truth

Listen to what I say
People of this great nation
We have the power to withstand
This poisoned oration

Just arise and tell the truth no matter the situation
The people
The place
Or the look on their faces
Do it in love
Because love will prevail over the rhetorical
Leaving peace, joy and unity as
Plentiful fruit for all to be edified

Scan the QR code with your phone and experience the video or audio of this poem performed by William Owens.

RESET

Sunday, October 16, 2016

Who am I?
Why am I?
What am I?
Where am I?
How did I evolve to the places and faces of the I that possesses my soul
That dictates a narrative
Trapping me in a vice of vicious conviction and condemnation?

As a nation, fighting off contamination of divisions too numerous to mention
Race, Sex, Creed, especially the Religion of what everyone believes to be the truth
Reasons of treasons to justify attacking one another rather than believing in God for a peace transcendent of who we are
For a quickening to be healed, made whole, transitioned into a transformed soul

As a man – in search of a fight to die for
Rising above the mundane exercise of existing to just make a living
As a woman – wanting to love and be loved by her hero
Contributing to all around her with the undying devotion of her wisdom and affection
Because we all need it

The purpose of my existence
The agony of stagnation – going nowhere
The reality of frustration – answers evade my mediations
The void is making more noise than all the music on every station – online and in the car – Pandora's box and XM satellite – and on my phone – the noise is deafening, got my head spinning, my heart vexed. I need a way to start afresh, to clear my head, my soul, my heart and what I think I believe – I need to reset

To reset is to forgive the ills of the past
Whose pet we've become when we sing that dead song
Before others I must forgive myself – for letting my heart drift through rifts of issues mostly not even my own

For judging with a stern finger in faces before me
They too are hurting
From this agony of poison
Creating confusion
Of who the real enemy is – it's not each other

Push the button now!

To reset is to rise up to ideas that capture sparks of love, the ability and agility of grace to endure, and power to change not found in me
It is to dance a romance of love throughout the galaxies past mere reality of the sometimes temporal illusions demanding me to believe they exist
Sing a song with rapturous melodies of divine infused

abilities that heal miraculously the hiding places of pain
that paralyzes my being
To reset is to speak truth with love unfeigned not trying to
prove a thang
Truth that makes the chains of never-ending blame melt
off from our brain
Freeing us to be realigned with true love... again

Push the button now!

Reset me God – show me how
To lose my life for Christ
To let go of my safe self
To become a conduit of Your power to heal, to love
To ascribe to Your kingdom and to Your will above

Reset me to release me
Reset me to realign me
Reset me to use me
Reset our nation
Reset our hearts
Nullify the division
We believe you, God

Push the button now!

****

Scan the QR code with your phone and experience the video or audio of this poem performed by William Owens.

THE RHYTHM OF THE LEAVES

Monday, October 17, 2016

Have you noticed the rhythm of the leaves?
How they move to the breeze with such ease
Never find them worrying, afraid of the night or the storming winds that come their way

They simply flow
No need to be afraid
They trust their creator and enjoy the season they've been given
Taking no thought for tomorrow
Just enjoying the breeze for the day

They catch the breeze that's for them
Celebrate the leaves that share their space
They together create a symphony of motion that's glorious
Just look at them...
They have a rhythm of unity
Not trying to be anything
Just being themselves
And flowing with the wind
Until their time comes to a graceful end

At the appointed time with beauty yet present
They change colors to bless us
With the season of autumn colors
They cover the earth
Giving the soil their soul
The joy soaked in from the sun

May we learn from them
And simply learn to flow in God's wind
And find our unity with each other
It is what we all need
This is what I learned this morning
From watching
The rhythm of the leaves

Scan the QR code with your phone and experience the video or audio of this poem performed by William Owens.

PERCEPTION

Tuesday, October 18, 2016

Reflect upon the issues of your heart
Found within the chambers of experiences you've had in life
Sometime hidden from you
In a crevice so deep
What you see is not true
It's a mere perception that has set your direction
Controlled your affections
Determine even your orientation
Will even predict your destination

America has subjugated her responsibility
To adapting this travesty
Our country tis of thee
Has lost her passion
Her direction
Her freedom
Her liberty

Only through truth
Rooted in love
Grounded in God
Can what we perceive the truth indeed

Intellect
Proper dialect

Can never interpret what is pure
It must be by faith in God
That our eyes are opened to see

Our job is not to judge, cast blame
only to remain in Him
For He alone has the power to give us
A truthful perception
of what is
what was
and what is to be...
His Will

HEMORRHAGE

Wednesday, October 19, 2016

Hemorrhage
Of heart
Of spirit
Of emotional damage done to our minds

Reflecting on times past
Not able to break free
We hemorrhage again and again
Only to repeat the same thing

What is this?
The repeat of the past
The trap of thinking, eating and drinking
The history of evil perpetrated by people
Bound to a demonic attack
This narrative of history must be placed upon the altar
Allow the fire of forgiveness to purge and set free
This alone will stop the Hemorrhaging

It's time to begin again and move upward
God is waiting

PURGE

Thursday, October 20, 2016

There is always the need to cleanse away
Dead leaves that are no longer
Fulfilling the need of the vine
There is always a call to purge
The thing that makes us fall
That clouds our sight from seeing truth

To gain one must lose the thing
Or the person who is denying you
Denying you from being the you God made you to be
From flowing and soaring with ease
As you pursue your destiny
So few know such life because they refuse
To rid themselves of the dead, dying
And defiled thing that's in their hand

Like America
She has found herself bound with the putrid worship of man
Should she return, there must be a purge of the filth
That has rifted her soul
Brought turmoil
Angst with pain from the past
Drinking dregs of regret
Feasting in the mess of relativity
Everyone doing what's right "to me"

Unless we are purged by sufferings
By the loss of what we've been trusting
We will be damned to an eternal positioning
Never able to receive grace to be saved...

Purge me, Lord
Purge the USA

Trouble is coming

I'M TIRED

Friday, October 21, 2016

I'm tired of the pain
I see on the faces of people
Who've been deceived
By the rhetoric of the elitist
Dumbed down by the tolerance of evil
Pillaged by economic manipulation
Drained from unnatural laws that are evil
I'm just tired

Seeing with eyes and grieved in heart
I've witnessed the atrocities of reckless lies
Damage precious lives
Deceive the simple people amongst us

Who need our protection
Depend on upright and genuine direction
That leads us all to search out the truth
I'm just tired

...too tired to even finish this

....
....
....

But Grace!
Gives me hope that makes me not ashamed.
Gives me resolve to stay in the race
Gives me a shield to quench every fiery flame
Sent to destroy my faith

As I yield and rest in Him
With no need to perform to dabble in sin
I am promised to win
Receive strength to mount up on wings like eagles
And get busy for the King

Where will America then stand?

PROVOKED

Saturday, October 22, 2016

Why are we so easily provoked
Becoming a kind of folk who do not reflect who we really are?

How have we become this way?
What persuaded us as a nation to become
A complaining, agitated union that thrives on division

We're destroying instead of building our communities
Rooted in a love that's founded and grounded beyond
The pale, stale, putrid fallen humanity that can't be what we need
For the heart is sick from the head to its feet

The evidence is beyond mere opinion
When diagnosed the condition is known by its symptoms
Irritable attitude
Impatient, no gratitude
Arrogant
Boastful no control
Mean spirited
Angry
Resentful
Even though successful

Yet when tried in the fire we are exposed to be outright pitiful
With all our abilities as a people
Called Americans
This is actually unbelievable

The remedy will not be what we think it'll be
Nor be found by doing more of "me"
Or even a collective "we"
Thinking our self-righteousness knows what to do
Knows what's best even though for decades
We've been there and done that
In fact, we're in a vicious cycle of familiarity
Thinking that the common will bring us liberty

We need more than that to neutralize or merely pacify
That's called compromise
America needs to be brought to genuine repentance
For her negligence of the truth
She'll never be soothed
Will always have the blues

Through repentance she'll have
Deliverance without performance
It shall break forth as the noon-day sun
Become a free-hearted people
No longer bound
Walking with a frown

Being men pleasers
Afraid to take a stand
Or to even make a friend
With one who has a different hue of skin
Because our eyes will be turned to Him
Our life is being seen as temporal
Our hope turned eternal

We then will understand
Our existence is not of ourselves
It belongs to the One
Who gave of Himself
For our freedom
Found in a purpose beyond
Our understanding

It is in these ways that we as a nation
Of tribes and people will be stoked
We will arise and become great perhaps for a season
We then will no longer be a band of mere mortals
Who subscribe to fear based living
We now thrive in building communities
Abound in a unity
That speaks a language that's universal
Seen by acts of compassion, waves of mercy
Not heard by mere words

We are immortals through Him
We will arise and invoke greatness
To never be provoked
By the base instincts of the lesser one inside us all

SIGH

Sunday, October 23, 2016

Why do we sigh throughout the day?
What is it that weighs upon our heart?
Why are we so concerned that it becomes a burden
Making it hard to breath
Instead we sometimes heave?

Then we sigh

It's our lungs telling us they too are tired
But the sigh is good
It's giving us a chance to reset
With extra oxygen to our brain.
Making us think deeper
Lest we go insane
Trying to refrain from losing it
Mostly over nothing

Because it never turns out the way we think it will
So the next time you are tempted to sigh... just breathe
And instead, just give God thanks...

Because He's in control of your life and even the USA

TIME

Monday, October 24, 2016

Time will teach you a thing or two
If you ignore it
Only you will lose
One way or another
Time will get its due

The question that we must address
Is will there be enough time for America to adjust?
For our nation to reset
For hearts to be mended
Tempers deflated

We need time to redeem
To redress the mess we have gotten ourselves in
Only the right kind of time will work this way
It will be the Father of time
That has mercy
Only then will time be released to work it
For our good

CONSCIENCE

Tuesday, October 25, 2016

I can't seem to find what has me roving around
The same light pole at the exact same time
What keeps me trippin' over the same problem
Agitated by the same people even though they're dead and gone

I find myself attracted to the same kind of woman
No... I'm not sleeping around
But they got this mindset that they can't make it
So sometimes I fake it
Kinda feel obligated to take them there as a friend
Then I keep on moving

I'm voting like I'm choking
Being forced to do what I've always done
No matter if my fav candidate got issues
This don't make sense
'Cause I feel guilty when I look over the fence
To vote against this
I mean it's hard to know deep inside my soul
I will yet vote for them
.... I guess

What's got me in bondage to this drama?
Almost eating my own vomit

'Cause I know I'm gone get sick
This is stupidddd!

I recently figured it out
It's the truth with no doubt
It's my conscience
That has me in this bondage

It ain't "The man"
Regardless of what he's done, doing or going to do
Ain't the government or a special interest group
No one brought me there
I came on my own because
I'm a slave to an eight year old

Forged and shaped since I was at least eight
Impressed and dressed to never think for myself
Religion reinforced to just pay attention on Sunday
With another thump on Wednesday
Then I was free to wander till my conscience
Was conditioned to believe that I was destined
To be that image deep inside my brain
Soon I became 18, 21, 29, 35
And now I'm a bit over 50
I was existing but knew
I wasn't really alive and living
Something was controlling my life from way deep inside
Voices speaking
Even Condemning

Unrelenting pressure to find that light pole
Take another stroll
Kick the person who hurt me
Not even thinking about forgiving

I'm sweating drops of acid
That disfigures my countenance for that moment
How come it's like this even as a God fearer
I claim I'm free
Yet act like I'm on detention
Guilty for nothing but accused
By the 8 year old still inside my mind

No wonder so many people are angry
Cursing God and don't know why
Go into a rage because they were looked at
A traffic light

We are all in a freefall of pain
Looking for some love, a hug, a friend
Shelter from the rain
That we ourselves put ourselves in

That little girl
That little boy
Who's only 8 has mastered us...
But it's not too late to change

It was this that made me realize that through
Christ I'm not only alive but free - way past my mind
But in my conscience especially

It says this in Hebrews 9:14
How much more shall the blood of Christ...
purge your conscience from dead works
To serve the living God.

As I read this as that 8 year old

Embedded inside my soul
Starting screaming, spitting and kicking
Even threatening me

My spirit shifted
Because I felt lifted just rereading this
Yea it was the Bible
But it starting to make sense
The connection was evident
Blood
Death
Life

It would take a new blood for a transfusion
Of the old blood that kept this eight year old talking inside
It would take a perfect death
In place of my death to make me alive
...that's called being born again

I said it with faith but this time out loud
THROUGH CHRIST BLOOD MY CONSCIENCE
IS PURGED FROM DEAD WORKS
TO SERVE THE LIVING GOD!

The voice of that eight year old
That old light pole
Begins to dissolve before my face
After a few days they were gone
Since then I'm a new man
No longer feeling less than
Guilty, dirty and unworthy

I don't even think of those things
I used to because they've been purged
Don't even have the urge
My time is spent in living the newness of life

Only found in and through the One
Who can purge to the depth of my conscience
He tasted death for me then became the resurrected Christ
I'm no longer eight

Scan the QR code with your phone and experience the video or audio of this poem performed by William Owens.

OH GOD

Wednesday, October 26, 2016

I'm screaming His name
When I think I'm losing control
Feel threatened, agitated
It could be that I'm elated

No matter what state I'm in
I simply think of Him
I center my affections
Whether because of acceptance or rejection
I give Him praise
He's the beginning of days
The end of everything

Oh God, I exclaim!
Oh God, I exclaim!

For you are my God
The God of this nation
The God of every nation
Regardless of man

Man that You made
In the image of Yourself
It's why we can't help but call Your name
Whether in reverence or in vain...

We cry, Oh God.

Answer us back in kindness
Remove the blindness
Fill the depth of our void
Silence the deafening noise

As we cry in our despair
To the One who resides above the galaxies and the stars
In the heavens of the heaven
Hear our cry
Oh God

BUMPS

Thursday, October 27, 2016

There are bumps not only
On the road on which I drive
But bumps in certain areas of my life
They serve to remind me
How much of others I need
Of God, especially

Some bumps make me bleed
Make me cry
Ask questions as to why
Where, how, who
Even what do I do

Bumps can come from neglect of our own
Bumps can even be the stuff of others' souls
Can't always know when or why
They just arrive and stop you in your stride

Yet bumps are critical for correcting
Even sometimes protecting us
From going too fast
Bumps make us slow down and focus
On what is really there
Unless we keep the press and eventually create a mess

Reflect carefully
Breathe deeply
The bump is there for a reason
Let it work God's purpose in your life
and even in our nation

Should we endure, it will bring a new-found
Freedom and an authentic liberation
All this from a bump

MY WHOLE HEART

Friday, October 28, 2016

I do give my whole heart
It's the only way to live and therefore to love
To thrive with no fear or regret
Accepting the grace I have to live with myself
No matter where I'm at or who gets me
Even rejects me
It's okay

I will still love myself and others
For it covers all our faults
Restores us each morning
To start again with a determination to win
This demands all of me

Beyond the me that I see, that I feel
Even beyond what the me in me believes
Belief rooted in anxieties
Forged from someone else's story
Instead of giving glory to God

The nation in which I live must reset and give
Give not riches that fade away

That adds no sunshine to one's day
She must find her heart

Begin to discover again what she's lost
...Her faith in God

Say what you will
Argue what you want
It would never be like this
If we didn't put God out of schools

Should our hearts go astray and be polluted
By envy and the pursuit of carnal pleasures
It will eventually die

The only safe place for our hearts
The only hope for our nation
Is to give our whole heart back to God

We will then find contentment
Rest for our weary souls and confused minds...

My whole Heart, Oh God
I give
I give
to Thee alone

THE FINISH LINE

Saturday, October 29, 2016

No one wins if they fail to keep
The finish line in mind
No one decides to take a hike or to ride a bike
Unless they have a plan to return
The finish line is crossed the minute you take off
It is done, but now you have to resolve
By faith to fulfill what you see
What you believe and to affirm it is so

The finish line is before you
Press on
Believe
Hold on
Never let go
Of the hope you have inside your soul
God is with you
With us throughout time

We must ever forget those things
That are behind us and that of our nation
Instead, let us embrace our neighbors
And communities in which we live
Together press toward and through the finish line
Before us

THE NEXT DAY

Sunday, October 30, 2016

The next day – behold it's upon you
Giving you new rays of sunshine
The soft dew in the morning time

Thoughts, ideas and a few concerns
...of course they all will come

A new day means you are alive
As you open your eyes the reality of life's...
Demands present themselves one at a time
Joys, moments of laughter
Hope, dreams and romantic pleasures
Are all treasures
That are opened
When the next day arrives

Our families
Our nation
Our communities
All live in expectation
Of what the next day will bring

May we look to Him who orchestrates
Every single thing
And simply believe
That our next day will always be a blessing.

A JOYOUS GAZE

Monday, October 31, 2016

I look upon the sun that has set
I see beyond the normal
I feel past the usual
I desire the divine presence of God

The hues touch me deep inside
Create an appetite to aspire to where God resides
I recognize
I contemplate
I attune myself to transition
To pay attention
To retain my passion

All this and more at the joyous gaze of the sun going down
I'm at peace

COMPOSURE

Tuesday, November 1, 2016

Composure is like roses
That bloom by being still in
The presence of the Lord
They struggle not

Have no fear as they rejoice
In their uniqueness
As they draw near to rise
Towards the one who has given them life
A life that blossoms

May we yield and discover the blessedness
In being still before the one
Who loves with perfect love

Resist the deceptive urge to let the enemy
Of your soul unnerve your spirit
As he seeks to distract
As to attract you to temptation
Found in a dark place that has no light

May we by grace remain in His Grip
For in doing so by His Spirit
We will know composure
In glorious expectation

Heavenly exaltation
May America through contemplation
Examine herself and by grace regain
Her composure and give God all the glory

I GOT TO

Wednesday, November 2, 2016

There are things that I just go to...
Do
See
Feel
Say
Go
and Be

There is a beckoning that lures my heart
Into ideas that won't let me rest
Thinking I have to just go there to be saved
To be assured that who I am yet is relevant

Truth be told, the only "got to" in life is God
Knowing Him and Him knowing me
Seeing Him pleased in my activity
Hearing His voice despite the noise
This is what I "got to"... what's yours?

I got to go pray
I got to go forward
I got to lift up my voice
For the truth
For my country to be saved
From enemies of our states

I got to make into heaven
With treasure awaiting

These are the real matters
In which to pay attention
All else only serves as a distraction
Got it?

THE FIELD OF BLOOD

Thursday, November 3, 2016

Precious ones are no more
Their souls have been transported
Into the bosom of God
Behind, their bodies are found
In the field of blood

Paid for by a ransom of betrayal
Of those closest to them
Of those through whom they came
Of those who unattached their limbs
Removed their feet and then their hands
They felt the incomprehensible pain

With nowhere to run
Their voice cannot plead for their hope to live
To take their first breath
To feed off their mother's breast

Blood spilled upon the fields
Purchased by the ransom given to those
Who betrayed the gift they were born to be

Instead they were removed by violence without notice
From the safest place – that it should be

The womb of mother – a divine cover
Protected with the strength of their father
Even animals defend their own and yet they have no soul

How could we – made in His image –
Yield to such violence
Execute one made in His image
With a touch of our DNA

Thirty pieces of silver
For a life of pleasure
A betrayal of our own selves
For the convenience to not be bothered

Compromise for reasons that cannot endure
The judgment that shall come
This is nothing but predetermined murder

From this field
Little souls shall arise
Be joined with their new bodies in the sky
Tears wiped from their eyes

You who have committed this act
Of treason and betrayal
Can be forgiven should you ask to
Be restored by His grace
Meet your little one in paradise

As they arise
From the field of blood

They are complete and in His presence
Soon to be given a resurrection from
The wretched field of blood
They will be restored as they enter into
The blessed hope of eternal life

Scan the QR code with your phone and experience the video or audio of this poem performed by William Owens.

BIRDS AT EASE

Friday, November 6, 2016

The birds jump up
Their wings take flight
Flying as high as they can
To share a line between poles with a fellow friend

Chirp and jump over one bird to get to the next
The birds are lined up waiting to eat again
A bird-size bite
No worries about what to eat or where to sleep
Just delight in the sun
The catch of the next worm

They think not about what will be
Have no idea of such things
They relish in the love of their creator
They simply expect Him to feed and provide for them

I will learn their song
Dance their dance
And worship as they do
And simply trust in Him
I'm worth more than them

Selah

GET FREE

Saturday, November 7. 2016

What but freedom matters to the soul of man
What is the what we search for that we call a plan

Is it not but for freedom?
It is!
It is!
Let it ring!
Let it ring!

I'm free!

THE FINISH LINE

Saturday, November 8. 2016

As I press through the line that was set before time for me
I do so with the prize in mind
Without guilt or regret
No blame
Or shame
Just a determined heart to say it is finished

It started at conception
However, it was before that as a reflection
In the mind of God
Who ends all things... but also starts them
Only He can say and said, "It is finished"

As I strive to complete what I see in my spirit
The turmoil of suffering
Of being alone
On the verge of losing my mind
Because the devil wants to destroy
Who I am before I cross that line

I know perhaps this truth can't be grasped
By those who've compromised themselves with a lie
And have blurred their finish line
Not I
I must remain sober

Let my chin shake beneath
The pressure
Shed a tear if I have to
It's okay

I will arise to embrace my destiny that awaits me
When I'm through I will hear God say, "Well done"

Then I'll say, "Through Him, it is finished!"

The following poems are selected poems that have been included in this book. They speak of issues that we must confront deep within our own hearts. Issues of refugees, being patient with ourselves and others, never giving up on what's true and right. If we refuse, for whatever reason we think we are justified, these issues will bleed out and trouble our communities and our nation even more.

I believe we must resist the powerful pull of groups, whether religious, political or social and ask God in childlike faith to show us as an individual... truth. Truth is not to be taught, nor is it transferable in its essence. One can sow seeds, others can water, but ultimately truth must kiss you itself with favor and then you will know it intimately.

You then will be free.

I pray these additional poems grip you as they have done to me,

William Owens

PERCEPTION

Reflect upon the issues of your heart
Found within the chambers of experiences you've had in life
Sometime hidden from you
In a crevice so deep
What you see is not true
It's a mere perception that has set your direction
Controlled your affections
Determine even your orientation
Will even predict your destination

America has subjugated her responsibility
To adapting this travesty
Our country 'tis of thee
Has lost her passion
Her direction
Her freedom
Her liberty

Only through truth
Rooted in love
Grounded in God
Can what we perceive truth indeed

Intellect
Proper dialect
Can never interpret what is pure

It must be with faith in God
That our eyes are opened to see

Our job is not to judge, cast blame
only to remain in Him
For He alone has the power to give us
A truthful perception
of what is
what was
and what is to be...
His Will

IMPLICIT TRUST

My heart shakes at the prospect
Of trusting you without a net
To give you all the things that I hoard
Inside my soul because deep in there
I'm afraid of letting go
Thinking that holding on makes me safe
I've yielded to a false narrative
Now I'm paralyzed with a fear that
Lives somewhere in my head

Rather than trust you, I chose to evade
Evade your love
Evade your care
Evade you with religious excuses
While yet praising your name

You are calling me with loving cord strings to implicit trust
To press beyond the stuff
I've allowed to become embedded in my thoughts
Clouding my heart from walking in childlike faith

There is a new place I have not seen
Words I have not heard
Experiences I've not had
Because I refuse to remove the net
To implicitly trust in your name

Implicit Trust
Brings rest
Allows vision to become clear
Boldness to arise in my heart
To speak forth truth without fear
To love and be loved without limit
Or resistance

Implicit Trust
Breaks forth in a new song
Dances a new dance
Makes loud the beat on the drum
Makes me transform into the person
You've purposed me to be and to become
Loving people and being loved

I will arise to this place
I will embrace your love
I will be the child of the highest
Without reservation

No need for explanation
In constant amazement
Of my heart
My purpose
The help of my nation

Without hesitation
With praise and adoration
Upon your love I do thrust myself
I do so day by day, moment by moment
In an open heart of filled with joy and implicit trust

Scan the QR code with your phone and experience the video or audio of this poem performed by William Owens.

I GOT TO

There are things that I just go to…
Do
See
Feel
Say
Go
and Be

There is a beckoning that lures my heart
Into ideas that won't let me rest
Thinking I have to just go there to be saved
To be assured that who I am yet is relevant

Truth be told the only "got to" in life is God
Knowing Him and Him knowing me
Seeing Him pleased in my activity
Hearing His voice despite the noise
This is what I "got to"… what's yours

I got to go pray
I got to go forward
I got to lift up my voice
For the truth
For my country to be saved
From enemies of our states

I got to make into heaven
With treasure awaiting

These are the real matters
In which to pay attention
All else only serves as a distraction
Got it?

PRESS

Press past the pain
Press through the rain
Don't let people drain you from
the God-given vision
He's called you to

There is a purpose
Beyond this realm of life
A purpose that fits you
like a tailored suit
That's zoot

So press
You can do this
...America

WAIT

In the midst of the storm
That whirls around your heart
Agitates your brain
Pushes you to insane places of imagination
That tempt you to be afraid...
Simply wait

Be still
In the midst of the impossibility that threatens you
To change your position of faith
You must simply be still
Even in the face of an impending threat
That wants you to retreat in defeat

Cast the imagination down
That is simply wanting to drag you around
To a no where that fears you of being now here
Where God is
Working
Performing
Bringing to pass His promise
Made to you before the foundations
Were established?

You must wait

Waiting is trusting
The deepest witness of loving
The one who loves you perfectly

He is working in your waiting
The train is coming
To take you to a place
That has not entered your mind

Waiting is a potent form of doing
For you are preparing to receive the promise
Possessing your soul in deep contemplation
Waiting is seasoning your heart to be imparted upon
The will of heaven

Even if death tells you not to
He has the keys
Does what He pleases
In the time that He has decreed before time became
Your waiting will not be in vain

The people who love this nation
Who pray for her deliverance
Must wait.... not too much longer
The Redeemer is coming
A new thing will happen
As you wait in joyful anticipation of steadfast faith

I say to you, WAIT...

****

Scan the QR code with your phone and experience the video or audio of this poem performed by William Owens.

REFUGEE

My eyes open in the morning
Seeking for redemption
From the agony of suffering in the grip of misery
Forced upon me as a refugee

Misplaced without reason
Abandoned to the treason of evil contrived by dark hearts
Bent on the death of innocence
Because of an inheritance of historic rhetoric

My skin I chose not
My eyes
My hair,
My voice are no less beautiful than yours

We breath the same air
My dreams for love
My hopes for a child in my chest
I rest from the sentence of this death
I cry to be free
To be seen as a human being
Not merely as a refugee

I speak not of those in faraway lands
Trapped by borders
Hemmed in by men with guns and axes

With wicked devices planned
I speak of my soul
Trapped within the control of vices
That make me bound, not free
In some ways we are all refugees

Seeking for a place to call home
To find rest
To reset
To quiet the cries of our loves ones near us
To bereave others hung on a cross before our faces
Raped and maimed
Left for dead
Even some I've seen beheaded

I at all costs will endure land and sea
For a chance at life
I'm driven
By the same reason as you
Desire for freedom
Hope for liberty
The dream of no longer being called a refugee

Death has no grip on me
Fear is prisoner of God's perfect love
I have sole faith Christ
Will rise above
Joy, not bound by hate
Redemption, mine by faith

We all are refugees in need
My eyes open in the morning
My heart is at peace within
I know through Him I'm free
No matter what land I'm in

I yield to His compassion made real – so real to me
As I do so to them
I have done so to Him
To do all I can to show His love to those
Who like me are refugees
That can be made free

****

Scan the QR code with your phone and experience the video or audio of this poem performed by William Owens.

Shift to Greatness!

The rift has ripped the core of our souls
And has blinded us to the gold inside of us
Refusing joy, the right to flow to and fro
Like a cold and cruel wind across our face
Blinding us to the beauty of every race
Dividing our nation that's the land of the free
And the home of the brave

We must shift from this madness
That has our hearts twisted
Because of a narrative
That once existed
A history whose purpose
Reaches beyond what we can grasp
Cease from your own understanding

Allow revelation of perfect symmetry and harmony
Capture your imagination
That will open your eyes to see a transition
Into God's eternal plan and destiny

A shift to greatness is as natural as
A smile of a child with no guile
A holding of lovers' hands strolling through the park
A transition of the sun so bright

To the glowing of the moon and stars
In the darkness of night

To shift is to resist the pull back to the insane drain
With drastic images of an evil past we make fresh
Again and again
Who wants bread from a microwave from last week
No matter how high the rise of the steam
Or how neat the butter looks in its cup
When the fresh bread is stale
Enough is enough

How long can we dwell on the evil of the past
Remaining blind
We deny ourselves to be
"Free at Last
Free at Last
Thank God Almighty
We're Free at Last"
The dream that Dr. Martin Luther King died for

Our grandmothers, grandfathers of decades gone by
Would see our day and ask us why...
"Haven't you done better?
If I had all this opportunity
Every day would be perfect weather
Why are you so easily played
By what people say
Or when they block you?

Child, you better straighten up your back
Smile and just push on through
To what God is calling you to"

Shifting with an intention to a purpose
Of greatness defines who you are
It's the ultimate high of life
The journey to the destination
The who of what God made you to be without apology
To shift is a radical transition
A denial of anyone or anything
Robbing you of your unique contribution
To the tapestry of your community
Yea... even to the grandeur of your very existence
Throughout the timeless reign of eternity
Let that sink deep into your spirit
Until alas you hear an intimate God-breathed epiphany

Transition is to smile at everyone
Regardless of who did what in times past
It is letting bygones be bygones
Because God still has a song for each us
Borne out of our journey to the shores
Of paradise with Christ

It is embracing the redemptive power of forgiveness
Loving your enemy regardless of their position
You see them through the same lens you see yourself
As great!

Transition requires looking deeper past the obvious
Expanding your heart and your love for all people
Thinking that lifts you to a new bold expression of faith
Tapping into that love that flows
From the depths of your DNA
Evidence that you where created with purpose
Beyond that of yourself

Purpose speaks to purpose
Greatness gives birth to greatness
We are connected to this objective
By the God of the universe that celebrates
All that's beautiful in us and through us to others

Shift to Greatness!
It's time to move beyond the line that blinds our eyes from
seeing inside the heart and mind of people who, like me,
bleed the crimson red that keeps us alive not dead

Shift to Greatness!
Press beyond the cynical syncs of souls
Who seek to hold you prisoner in a sick matrix of
Poisoned narratives that paralyze and ostracize you
From the perfect love of God
Draining you into a weathering shell of chaff
Blown by the winds of hate
With twisted faces
Disjointed legs
Going nowhere

Creating despair from hopelessness
Making themselves irrelevant to anything beautiful

God is calling you
God has purposed you
Ordained
Created
Loved, loves, and will forever love you perfectly

You must chose
You must decide
Whether you will live or die
Remain where you are
Or Rise and Resist
To fight for WHO God has made you to be
A transition to radically change your position
With heart, mind, and soul
fearless
Today is the day
For you
For America
For our communities
And every nationality
To...
SHIFT
to Greatness!

SHIFT TO GREATNESS

Follow William on his National
Shift to Greatness Bike Trek
www.shifttogreatness.com

****

Scan the QR code with your phone and experience the video or audio of this poem performed by William Owens.

Naked Before God

Words that Express My Heart
By William Owens

$19.95

www.throughpeople.com

Scan to Order: